HORSES

by Seymour Simon

HarperCollinsPublishers

Horses have always been very much a part of human life. During the last Ice Age, tens of thousands of years ago, people made cave drawings of horses. Today people create movies and books about horses.

More than five thousand years ago, early peoples tamed and herded horses on the grassy plains of Europe and Asia. During the ancient Babylonian, Greek, and Roman civilizations, people trained horses to draw their war chariots. Genghis Khan conquered Asia and eastern Europe with an army of a quarter of a million horsemen. Horses carried medieval knights and their armor into battle. The cowboys, the Native Americans of the western plains, and their horses were an important part of American history.

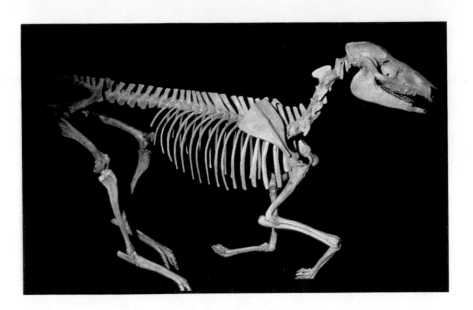

The ancestor of the horse, *Hyracotherium*, which means "mole beast," lived about fifty-five million years ago in the forests of what is now Europe and eastern Asia. It looked only slightly like the horses we know today. It was about the size of a spaniel and ate the leaves of trees. This small horse is also called *Eohippus*, which means "dawn horse."

Over tens of millions of years, horses slowly changed. *Mesohippus*, which means "middle horse," was the size of a large dog, about two feet high (shown above). It ate both tree leaves and grasses.

About ten million years ago, the first single-toed or single-hoofed horse roamed the plains of Europe and Asia. It was about as big as a pony and ate only grasses. *Equus*, the modern-day horse, appeared about two million years ago and is found over much of the world.

A horse's mouth is full of strong teeth used mostly for chewing and grinding grasses. Baby horses, called foals, have a full set of milk teeth when they are about nine months old, just like your baby teeth. Gradually the foals lose their milk teeth and grow permanent teeth. Over time, they wear down and change in shape and color.

The most accurate way to tell a horse's age is by looking at its teeth and gums. This is why we use the expression "from the horse's mouth," which means "from the original source." It would not be a good idea for you to guess a horse's age by opening its mouth. Unless you're an expert, you may be bitten.

Horses can see, hear, and smell. They have larger eyes than most other animals. Since a horse's eyes are set on each side of its head, it can see in almost a complete circle and can look around while grazing. Horses can see some colors, such as yellow and green, but they cannot see all the colors you can see.

Horses can hear both lower- and higher-pitched sounds than humans can. They move their ears to pick up faint sounds people cannot hear.

Horses can smell other animals and people up close and from far away. They can taste sweet foods. They love sugar or fruits, such as watermelon. Horses are also sensitive to touch. They can sense a fly landing anywhere on their bodies.

In spring or early summer, female horses, mares, mate with male horses, stallions. After about eleven months, a foal is born. Most births take place at night. When she is ready to give birth, the mare lies down. The foal usually is delivered in about fifteen minutes. A young mare is called a filly, and a young male is called a colt.

Right after the delivery, the mare gets up and licks her foal all over. In less than one hour, a foal is walking. It keeps in contact with its mother by bumping into her.

Horses don't talk of course, but they communicate in other ways. They recognize each other by their scent. Friendly horses often groom each other by nuzzling their manes and necks.

A horse moves its eyes and ears to show what it is feeling. When a horse lays back its ears and shows the whites of its eyes, it is angry or frightened. When the horse points its ears forward, it is interested in some object. When the horse lowers its ears, it is relaxed or sleeping. You can also tell that a horse is upset when it stamps a hind leg, shakes its head, and swishes its tail. Horses also make sounds such as neighing, nickering, and snorting. The sounds seem to show how the horse is feeling.

Stallions try to show who is dominant (the leader) by fighting, rearing, and stabbing their front hooves or biting the neck of the other horse.

Horses can sense when people are frightened or angry, perhaps by their smell. Touching, patting, and grooming build trust between a human and a horse.

Horses move in four natural ways, called gaits or paces. They walk, trot, canter, and gallop. The walk is the slowest gait and the gallop is the fastest.

When a horse walks, each hoof leaves the ground at a different time. It moves one hind leg first, and then the front leg on the same side; then the other hind leg and the other front leg. When a horse walks, its body swings gently with each stride.

When a horse trots, its legs move in pairs, left front leg with right hind leg, and right front leg with left hind leg. When a horse canters, the hind legs and one front leg move together, and then the hind legs and the other foreleg move together.

The gallop is like a much faster walk, where each hoof hits the ground one after another. When a horse gallops, all four of its hooves may be flying off the ground at the same time.

Horses are usually described by their coat colors and by the white markings on their faces, bodies, legs, and hooves.

Brown horses range in color from dark brown bays and chestnuts to golden browns, such as palominos, and lighter browns, such as roans and duns.

Partly colored horses are called pintos or paints. Colorless, pure-white horses—albinos—are rare. Most horses that look white are actually gray.

Skewbalds have brown-and-white patches. Piebalds have black-and-white patches. Spotteds have dark spots on a white coat or white spots on a dark coat.

Horses also vary in shape and size. Horses that look very much alike belong to the same breed. Just as spaniels, terriers, and collies are all still dogs, Arabians, Clydesdales, and mustangs are all still horses.

There are three groups of horse breeds—hotbloods, coldbloods, and warmbloods. Hotbloods originally came from the countries of North Africa and the Middle East, where the climate is hot. Coldbloods originally came from the countries of northern Europe, where the climate is cooler. A warmblood is the offspring of mating a hotblood and a coldblood.

Dating back more than forty-five hundred years, the Arabian is probably the oldest and best known of all the hotblood breeds. It is a small but tough horse.

Hundreds of years ago, Arabians were crossed with native English breeds to produce the Thoroughbred, the fastest and most expensive horse breed. Thoroughbreds are used in racing, steeplechasing, and other sports.

Coldblood breeds are large, heavy horses known for their calmness and patience. For centuries, Europeans used a particular coldblood breed to do farmwork and to pull heavy wagons.

The Shire is the biggest of the English coldbloods. It weighs as much as 2,200 pounds, more than the combined weight of all the students in your class. A pair of Shires is able to pull a load of 50 tons—about the weight of ten elephants.

Clydesdales are a bit smaller and lighter in weight than Shires. Clydesdales were used to plow the huge wheat fields and cornfields of the midwestern United States and central Canada.

Most of the horses we use are warmbloods. Contest or sporting horses are developed specifically for riding or jumping in sports such as polo. In polo, players mounted on horses use a long-handled mallet to try to hit a ball through goal posts. A polo pony is a Thoroughbred that's fast and tough and can change direction quickly.

In jumping or steeplechasing competitions, horses and riders jump over barriers or obstacles. Dressage is a competition in which a rider's hands, legs, and weight shift to guide the horse through a series of complicated movements. Competition training takes a great deal of time and effort, and a trained horse is very highly valued.

Ponies look different from horses. They are smaller, and they have short and usually hairy legs, sturdy bodies, and thick manes and tails. Horses and ponies are measured in *hands*, and each hand is about 4 inches. A pony is less than 14.2 hands high, about 57 inches.

The Dartmoor is a strong, tough pony that can carry a grown person. Some ponies live wild on the high open lands of Dartmoor, England. Their thick coats and shaggy manes and tails protect them in cold weather.

In the United States, there are many pony breeds, including the feral Chincoteague horses on Assateague, an island off the coast of Virginia; the Rocky Mountain; the Pony of the Americas; and the American Shetland, the most popular pony in the country. Today, there are about forty thousand Shetland ponies registered in the United States.

Feral horses are horses that were once tamed by people but have escaped back into nature. Mustangs are feral horses that live in the dry deserts of the American Southwest. They are protected so that they can continue to live "wild."

Camargue horses are feral horses that live in the swampy marshlands of southern France. In Britain, feral ponies live in the wild woodlands and moors.

Nearly five hundred years ago, horses were brought to America by Spanish explorers. The Europeans used their horses to help battle the Native Americans, and for trading purposes. Some horses escaped and lived in the wild.

By the 1600s, wild horses had spread over much of the American grasslands. Native Americans from the Sioux, Cheyenne, Comanche, Crow, and Pawnee peoples became the mounted buffalo hunters and warriors of the Great Plains. They could shoot arrows while galloping bareback on their horses and were excellent riders. So were the cowboys of the Old West.

In the 1800s, horses were used to transport settlers traveling westward across America in wagon trains, groups of horse-drawn covered wagons called prairie schooners. For centuries, horses have played a vital role in American history.

Modern industry would not have been possible without the use of horse-power. Before the invention of steam engines and gasoline engines, horses turned the wheels that provided power for machines in factories. This is how products such as cotton materials, flour, and iron were manufactured.

Horses pulled barges along canals and hauled fire engines, wagons, stage-coaches, and buses. In mines and forests, horses carried ore and logs. Like most Amish people, this lady still uses a horse-drawn plow.

Today, machines mainly do the work that horses once did. But "horsepower" is still the term used to measure the pulling strength of a car, train, or plane engine. It seems that horses will always be with people in one way or another.

At one time, most children who grew up on a farm or in the city learned how to care for a horse. Nowadays, few people ride horses, and even fewer own them.

Just like people, a horse needs to be given food, water, and shelter. It needs to be groomed, cleaned, and cared for. It needs to be shod. It needs regular exercise. In return, a horse can give us a wonderful feeling of close companionship and trust. And that's enough for true horse lovers.

For Chloe, Jeremy, Benjamin, and Joel,
with love from Grandpa

Special thanks to Patrick Thomas, Ph.D., Curator of Mammals, Bronx Zoo,
Wildlife Conservation Society, for his expert advice.

Photo credits: Front & back endpapers © 2003 Elisabeth Weiland / Photo Researchers, Inc.; pp. 4–5 © Alan Carey / Photo Researchers, Inc.; pp. 6–7 © Wolfgang Bayer / Bruce Coleman, Inc.; p. 7 (inset): © Douglas Mazonowicz / Bruce Coleman, Inc.; p. 8 © Alex Kerstitch / Visuals Unlimited, Inc.; p. 9 © 2003 Elisabeth Weiland / Photo Researchers, Inc.; p. 11 © 2005 Sylvain Cordier / Photo Researchers, Inc.; p. 12 © Rolf Kopfle / Bruce Coleman, Inc.; pp. 14–15 © Dusty Perin / Dembinsky Photo Associates; p. 17 © 2005 Henry Ausloos / Photo Researchers, Inc.; p. 18 © 2005 Connie Bransilver / Photo Researchers, Inc. ; pp. 20–21 © 2005 Art Wolfe / Photo Researchers, Inc.; p. 22 © 2005 Jerry Irwin / Photo Researchers, Inc.; p. 24 © Harry Cutting / Animals Animals; p. 25 © Charles Palek / Animals Animals; p. 26 © 2005 Gerry Cranham / Photo Researchers, Inc.; p. 27 © 2005 Explorer / Photo Researchers, Inc.; p. 28 © 2005 Kees Van Den Berg / Photo Researchers, Inc.; pp. 30–31: © Eastcott / Momatiuk / Animals Animals; pp. 32–33 © 2005 F. Stuart Westmorland / Photo Researcheers, Inc.; p. 35 © E. R. Degginger / Dembinsky Photo Associates; p. 37 © Sharon Cummings / Dembinsky Photo Associates.

ISBN   978-0-544-10321-4

9 10 0877 21 20 19 18 17 16 15 14

4500470499   A B C D E F G